Mississippi

BY ANN HEINRICHS

Content Adviser: Mary Beth Farrell, Instructor, Department of History, University of Southern Mississippi, Hattiesburg, Mississippi

Reading Adviser: Dr. Linda D. Labbo, Department of Reading Education, College of Education, The University of Georgia

COMPASS POINT BOOKS MINNEAPOLIS, MINNESOTA

Compass Point Books
3109 West 50th Street, #115
Minneapolis, MN 55410

Visit Compass Point Books on the Internet at *www.compasspointbooks.com*
or e-mail your request to *custserv@compasspointbooks.com*

On the cover: The American Queen riverboat on the Mississippi River

Photographs ©: Buddy Mays/Travel Stock, cover, 1, 19, 32; John Elk III, 3, 6, 21, 22, 26, 35, 37, 38, 39, 40, 41, 42, 43 (top), 45; Photo Network/Vic Bider, 4; Thomas R. Fletcher, 8; Robert McCaw, 9, 10, 44 (top, middle); Corbis Sygma/Sun Herald, 11; Hulton/Archive by Getty Images, 12, 15, 16, 18, 30; North Wind Picture Archives, 13, 14; DVIC/National Archives, 17, 47; Linda Saxon Nix, 2001, 20; Index Stock Imagery/Ralph Krubner, 24; Corbis/Philip Gould, 25, 28; USDA/ARS/Ken Hammond, 27, 48 (top); Getty Images/Arnaldo Magnani, 29, 46; Getty Images Inc./Keith D. Bedford, 31; Corbis/Kelly/Mooney Photography, 33; Getty Images/Al Bello, 34; Robesus, Inc., 43 (state flag); One Mile Up, Inc., 43 (state seal); PhotoDisc, 44 (bottom).

Editors: E. Russell Primm, Emily J. Dolbear, and Patricia Stockland
Photo Researchers: Marcie C. Spence
Photo Selector: Linda S. Koutris
Designer/Page Production: The Design Lab/Jaime Martens
Cartographer: XNR Productions, Inc.

Library of Congress Cataloging-in-Publication Data
Heinrichs, Ann.
   Mississippi / by Ann Heinrichs.
        p. cm. — (This land is your land)
 Summary: Introduces the geography, history, government, people, culture, and attractions of Mississippi. Includes bibliographical references and index.
   ISBN 0-7565-0355-8 (alk. paper)
   1. Mississippi—Juvenile literature. [1. Mississippi.] I. Title. II. Series.
   F341.3.H45 2004
   976.2—dc21   2003005407

Table of Contents

NOTE: In this book, words that are defined in the glossary are in **bold** *the first time they appear in the text.*

▲ **The historic Longwood mansion in Natchez**

Settlers poured into Mississippi in the early 1800s. The territory was famous for its rich soil. One settler said it "yields such noble crops that any man is sure to succeed." In time, cotton was "king" among Mississippi crops.

Reminders of the past are everywhere in Mississippi. Cotton **plantations** thrived before the Civil War (1861–1865). Many large homes remain from that time. Monuments and battlefields honor those who fought in the war. Mississippi's history is full of **civil rights** struggles, too. African-Americans spent many painful years seeking equal rights.

Television star Oprah Winfrey is just one of several famous Mississippians. Another is B. B. King, called the King of the Blues. Then there's Elvis Presley—the King of Rock and Roll.

Mississippi is still a leading farm state. Its **industries** now range from making furniture to testing rockets. Visitors enjoy the state's historic sites, beaches, and pine woods. Come explore Mississippi, and you'll enjoy it, too!

Rivers, Hills, and Plains

▲ The Mississippi River near Natchez

Mississippi is one of America's southern states. It's in a region often called the Deep South. Alabama lies along Mississippi's eastern edge. To the north is Tennessee. Arkansas and Louisiana are on the west. Louisiana also borders part of southern Mississippi. The rest of the southern border faces the Gulf of Mexico.

The mighty Mississippi River forms most of Mississippi's western border. Actually, the state was named after the river. *Mississippi* is a Native American word. It means "great waters" or "father of waters."

Most of Mississippi lies within the Gulf Coastal Plain. This is a low-lying region of plains and rolling hills. Many rivers cut across the state. Alongside these rivers are fertile lowlands called river bottoms.

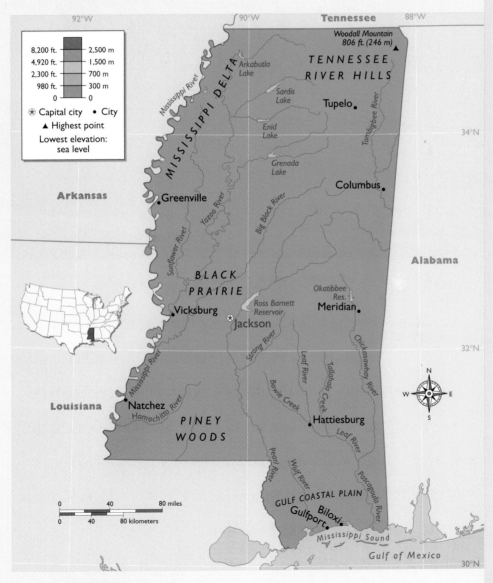

8,200 ft. — 2,500 m
4,920 ft. — 1,500 m
2,300 ft. — 700 m
980 ft. — 300 m
0 — 0

✹ Capital city   • City
▲ Highest point
Lowest elevation:
   sea level

92°W
90°W
Tennessee
88°W

Woodall Mountain
806 ft. (246 m) ▲

TENNESSEE
RIVER HILLS

Mississippi River
MISSISSIPPI DELTA
Arkabutla Lake

Sardis Lake
Tupelo.

Tombigbee River

34°N

Enid Lake

Grenada Lake

Columbus.

Arkansas

.Greenville

Yazoo River

Big Black River

Alabama

Sunflower River

BLACK PRAIRIE

Okatibbee Res.

.Vicksburg

Ross Barnett Reservoir

Meridian.

✹ Jackson

Strong River

Chickasawhay River

32°N

Mississippi River

Leaf River

Tallahala Creek

Louisiana

.Natchez

Homochitto River

Bowie Creek

PINEY WOODS

.Hattiesburg

Leaf River

Pearl River

Wolf River

Pascagoula River

0   40   80 miles
0   40   80 kilometers

GULF COASTAL PLAIN
Biloxi.
Gulfport.

N
W   E
S

Mississippi Sound

Gulf of Mexico

30°N

▲ A topographic map of Mississippi

▲ **A forest along the Yazoo River in western Mississippi**

The Mississippi Delta, or simply the Delta, is located in the northwest part of the state. Soil in the Delta is deep, black, and fertile. Over hundreds of years, the river left rich material there. The Delta used to suffer terrible floods. Now levees, or high walls, help hold back the river waters.

Southeastern Mississippi is called the Piney Woods. Its rolling hills are thick with pine forests. The Black Prairie is north of the Piney Woods. Like the Delta, it has rich, black soil. Many cotton plantations once spread across this area. Mississippi's northeastern corner is the state's highest region. Its forested slopes are the Tennessee River Hills.

Sandy beaches line Mississippi's coast. Several little bays cut into the coastline. Herons and other birds nest in the coastal **marshes.** Other coastal creatures are crabs, oysters, shrimp, and clams.

Just beyond the coast is a string of islands. They're protected as the Gulf Islands National Seashore. Squid, dolphins, and even whales live in the surrounding waters.

▲ Birds like the green heron nest in Mississippi's coastal marshes.

Huge magnolia trees with sweet-smelling flowers grow in Mississippi. The magnolia is both the state tree and the state flower. Forests cover more than half the state. Their pine trees have given Mississippi a booming lumber industry. Raccoons, opossums, foxes, and deer roam through the forests.

Mississippi's climate is warm and wet. Rainfall is heavy, especially in the south. Winters are short, and they are not usually very cold. Once in a great while, snow may fall.

▲ Raccoons live in Mississippi's many forests.

▲ These telephone lines were blown down by the strong winds of a hurricane that hit Mississippi.

Summers are hot throughout the state. The highest summer temperatures are in the Delta. Hurricanes sometimes hit the coast in the summer and early fall. Their fierce winds blow in from the Gulf of Mexico.

▲ A Choctaw camp on the Mississippi River

Mississippi was once home to thousands of Native Americans. The Natchez people lived in what is now southwest Mississippi. They grew corn, beans, and squash. They also got food by hunting, fishing, and gathering wild plants. The Natchez built huge mounds of earth. On top were buildings for religious ceremonies.

Central Mississippi was home to the Choctaw people. They were deer hunters and warriors. The Chickasaw lived in the north and east. They built their villages along rivers and streams. The men hunted deer, bears, and buffalo. Women tended the fields of crops.

Hernando de Soto of Spain was the first European in Mississippi. He explored the area from 1540 to 1541. In 1682, the French explorer René-Robert Cavelier, Sieur de La Salle, came down the Mississippi River. He claimed the river valley, including Mississippi, for France.

▲ René-Robert Cavelier, Sieur de La Salle (standing), and his companions on the Mississippi River in 1682

Pierre le Moyne founded a French settlement at present-day Ocean Springs in 1699. His brother Jean Baptiste established today's Natchez in 1716. Thousands of French settlers soon moved into the area. They raised tobacco, rice, and **indigo** on plantations. They brought in Africans to work as slaves in their fields.

Mississippi would pass to several countries. It became British territory in 1763. Spain took over the Gulf Coast area in 1781. After the Revolutionary War (1775–1783), Britain's land went to the United States. Mississippi became a U.S. territory in 1798. It finally was granted statehood in 1817.

▲ Pierre le Moyne and his brother established French settlements in Mississippi.

A route called the Natchez Trace connected Mississippi and Tennessee. Many pioneers took this trail into Mississippi. New settlers wanted to farm the Native Americans' lands. By treaties or by force, most of the Native Americans were removed.

Meanwhile, cotton had become the region's major crop. Throughout the South, slaves worked on the cotton plantations. However, Northern states were against slavery. This conflict would tear the nation apart. In 1861, Mississippi and

▲ **An expedition on the Mississippi River during the Revolutionary War**

other Southern states seceded, or left the Union. They formed the Confederate States of America. Union and Confederate forces fought the Civil War.

In Mississippi, bloody battles raged at Corinth, Vicksburg, and other sites. The Battle of Vicksburg helped the Union win the war. U.S. troops occupied Mississippi during **Reconstruction** and the freed slaves gained many rights. They quickly lost those rights, however, when Reconstruction ended.

▲ A Civil War battle at Corinth in October 1862

▲ These women worked as welders for a shipbuilding company in Pascagoula during World War II.

The early 1900s were hard on Mississippians. In 1907, insects called boll weevils destroyed much of the cotton crop. The Mississippi River flooded in 1927, leaving thousands homeless. State leaders helped their citizens by encouraging new industry, but the state remained poor. The Great Depression of the 1930s caused poverty throughout the United States. In Mississippi, many people lost their land and were out of work. World War II (1939–1945), however, created jobs for Mississippians. The state produced ships and other war supplies.

▲ In September 1962, James Meredith became the first black student to attend classes at the University of Mississippi. He had to be escorted by federal marshals because of rioters.

Mississippi suffered several racial conflicts in the 1960s. In 1962, James Meredith was the first black student to enter the University of Mississippi. This caused riots to break out. Civil rights champion Medgar Evers was killed in 1963. The next year, three civil rights workers were murdered near Philadelphia, Mississippi. Violence against people fighting for civil rights continued throughout the 1960s. Still, many ordinary people risked their lives to help others gain equal rights. By 1969, all of Mississippi's public schools were **integrated.** Today, Mississippi has many African-American elected government officials.

Mississippi continued to develop new businesses. They ranged from furniture making to catfish farming. Tourism became an important industry, too. Still, Mississippians' income and education levels were among the nation's lowest. State leaders are working hard to improve life for all their people.

▲ Riding the schooners at the Maritime and Seafood Industry Museum in Biloxi is a major tourist attraction.

▲ **The magnolia blossom became the state flower in 1952.**

Even children can take part in their government. In Mississippi, schoolchildren were asked to vote for two state symbols—the state flower and the state tree. In both votes, the magnolia won.

The magnolia tree became the official state tree in 1938. In 1952, the creamy-white magnolia blossom became the state flower. The children proved how important voting is. It gives citizens a voice in their own government.

Mississippi's state government is divided into three branches—legislative, executive, and judicial. Each branch has a special job to do. The United States government is organized the same way.

The job of the legislative branch is to make state laws. The lawmakers also decide how the state's money will be spent. Mississippi voters elect lawmakers to serve in the state

▲ **The state capitol in Jackson**

▲ Members of the state senate meet in this chamber in Jackson.

legislature. It's divided into two houses, or sections. One is
the 52-member senate. The other is the 122-member house of
representatives. They all meet in the state capitol in Jackson.

The executive branch's job is to carry out the state's laws.
Mississippi's governor is the head of the executive branch.

Voters elect a governor every four years. They also elect other important executive officials. The governor and lieutenant governor may serve only two terms in a row.

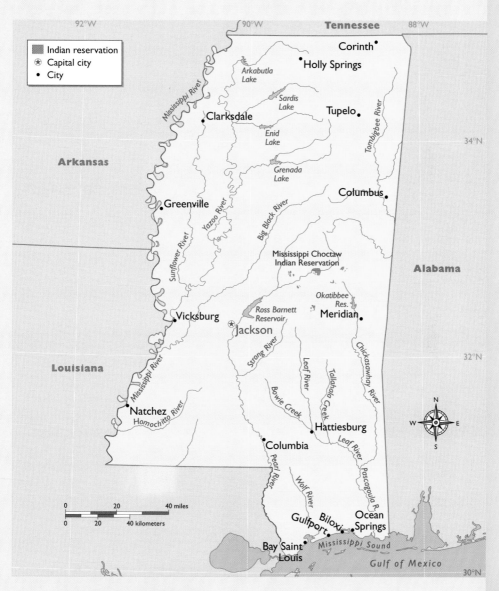

▲ **A geopolitical map of Mississippi**

The judicial branch decides whether laws have been broken. This branch is made up of judges. They hear cases in court and make their decisions. Mississippi's highest court is the state supreme court. Its nine justices, or judges, are elected to eight-year terms.

Mississippi is divided into eighty-two counties. Each county, in turn, is divided into five districts. Voters in each district elect someone to serve on their county's board of supervisors. Each county's five-person board takes care of county business. Most cities and towns elect a mayor and a council.

For a long time, Mississippians were loyal to the Demo-

▲ **Judges decide cases in this Jackson courthouse.**

cratic Party. However, in 1991, they elected Republican Kirk Fordice as governor. He was the first Republican governor since 1874.

Some Mississippians broke away from the Democratic Party in 1948. They joined other southerners in forming the Dixiecrat Party. Dixiecrats opposed national civil rights laws. They believed the states should make their own decisions about civil rights. However, the Dixiecrat Party soon died out.

▲ Civil rights activists were commemorated in Philadelphia on the twenty-fifth anniversary of the Civil Rights Act.

▲ Cotton continues to be a leading crop in Mississippi.

Cotton was once "king" in Mississippi's economy. Today, Mississippi farmers raise many valuable products. Cotton is still the leading crop, followed by soybeans. Rice, corn, and sweet potatoes are important crops, too. However, chickens bring in the most farm income. Mississippi is a leader in producing broilers, or young chickens. Many farmers also raise dairy cattle, beef cattle, and hogs.

The Delta region is Mississippi's richest farming area. You might be surprised at one of its "farm" products—catfish! Mississippi is America's top producer of farm-raised catfish.

By the 1960s, manufacturing had become Mississippi's major industry. Today, food products are the state's leading factory goods. Food plants process chickens, eggs, milk, and fish. They bake cakes and make soft drinks. Other factories make chemicals such as medicines and fertilizer. Car and truck parts and huge ships are also made in Mississippi.

Mississippi's forests provide wood that is used for many different purposes. Some trees are sawed into lumber for building houses. Other trees are made into furniture or paper. Pine trees also yield turpentine, tar, and pitch.

▲ Workers harvesting catfish in the Delta region

▲ Service workers in Metcalf, including the mayor (front, center), firefighters, and a police officer

Petroleum (oil) and natural gas are Mississippi's top mining products. The richest oil deposits are in the southeast and southwest. Other valuable minerals are clay, limestone, sand, and gravel.

Service industries employ more Mississippians than any other business. Service jobs include positions in health care, teaching, banking, and repair. Service people may also work in hotels, restaurants, and grocery stores. Thousands of people are employed by the state's gambling casinos. Others work on military bases or at the Stennis Space Center. They all provide important services to others.

Where did Oprah Winfrey and Elvis Presley come from? The answer is Mississippi! When it comes to entertainment, they're Mississippi's biggest stars. Oprah is the most popular talk-show host in the United States. Elvis is known worldwide as the King of Rock and Roll.

It's amazing to see how many famous people came from Mississippi. Many of them are well-known musicians. They include country music singers Charley Pride, LeAnn Rimes, Conway Twitty, and Tammy Wynette.

▲ **Famous Mississippian Oprah Winfrey hosts a national talk show in Chicago.**

▲ Performer Muddy Waters was famous for helping create the Delta blues.

The opera star Leontyne Price also came from Mississippi.

B. B. King and Muddy Waters helped create the Delta blues. That's a style of blues music from the Mississippi Delta. Their songs tell of sad times, hard luck, or broken hearts. Even their guitars "sing the blues." Delta bluesmen make the strings whine like a human voice.

The deep-voiced actor James Earl Jones is a Mississippian. Writers Tennessee Williams and William Faulkner were, too. Faulkner's stories all take place in a **mythical** Mississippi county. Don't forget Jim Henson.

He created the Muppets—Miss Piggy, Kermit the Frog, and their friends.

In 2000, there were 2,844,658 people in Mississippi. That made it thirty-first in population among all the states. Jackson, the state capital, is the largest city. Next in size are Gulfport, Biloxi, and Hattiesburg.

Before 1940, African-Americans made up more than half the population. Today, more than one out of three residents is black. No other state has a larger proportion of African-Americans in its population.

About three out of five Mississippians are white. Many have roots in England, Ireland, and other European countries. Most of the state's Native Americans belong to the Choctaw tribe. Chinese, Southeast Asian, and **Hispanic** people live in Mississippi, too.

▲ Actor James Earl Jones is from Mississippi.

More than half of all Mississippians live in rural areas. Those are areas outside of cities and towns. The Delta region has the biggest rural population. Many people there are poor.

On the Gulf Coast, shrimp fishing is a big industry. Every June, Biloxi holds the colorful Blessing of the Fleet ceremony. First, a wreath is thrown into the water. This honors shrimp fishers who have been lost at sea. Then, dozens of shrimp boats parade by. A priest blesses them, praying for their safety.

▲ **Shrimp boats in the water near Biloxi**

▲ Couples dressed in clothes from the mid-1800s dance during the Natchez Spring Pilgrimage.

The Natchez Spring Pilgrimage is a monthlong festival. People tour elegant homes built before the Civil War, with ladies in hoopskirts as their hosts. The evenings are filled with live performances. Many other communities hold this type of festival, too.

Greenville presents the Mississippi Delta Blues and Heritage Festival. It's the biggest blues festival in the South. Besides the music, people enjoy delicious, home-style cooking.

Football season is an exciting time in Mississippi. Everyone takes sides for the season's big event. That's when the University of Mississippi Rebels take on the Mississippi

▲ Green Bay Packer Brett Favre is from Mississippi.

State Bulldogs. Many professional football stars came from
Mississippi. One is Brett Favre, the quarterback for the Green
Bay Packers. Another was Walter Payton of the Chicago Bears.

Let's Explore Mississippi!

▲ **A cannon at Pascagoula's Old Spanish Fort**

Mississippi is full of surprises and new things to learn. You'll discover historic sites and nature trails. You'll even explore the space age!

Would you like to travel to Mars, land a space shuttle, or visit a space station? You'll have all this **virtual** fun at the Stennis Space Center. It's the United States' largest test station for rockets. You'll find it on the coast near Bay Saint Louis.

Pascagoula, Biloxi, and Gulfport are the main Gulf Coast cities. Pascagoula's Old Spanish Fort dates from 1718. From Gulfport, you can hop on a boat to the Gulf islands.

Gulf Islands National Seashore lies just off the coast. Most of its islands are natural and wild. You'll enjoy their snow-white beaches and sparkling blue waters. Crabs and beach

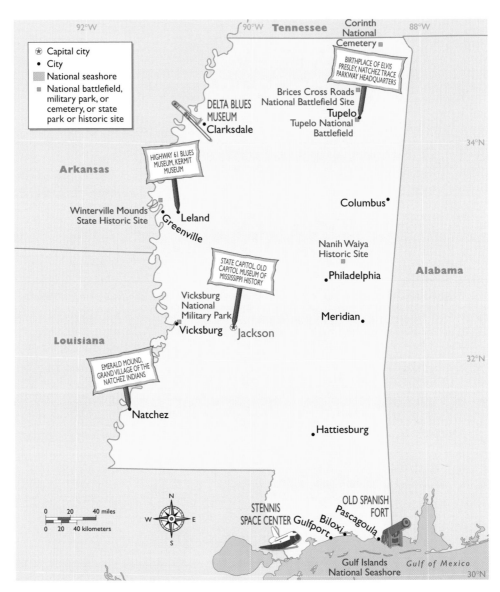

Legend:
- ✪ Capital city
- • City
- ▨ National seashore
- ▪ National battlefield, military park, or cemetery, or state park or historic site

92°W · 90°W · 88°W

Tennessee

Corinth National Cemetery ▪

BIRTHPLACE OF ELVIS PRESLEY, NATCHEZ TRACE PARKWAY HEADQUARTERS

Brices Cross Roads National Battlefield Site

DELTA BLUES MUSEUM
• Clarksdale

Tupelo•
Tupelo National Battlefield

34°N

Arkansas

HIGHWAY 61 BLUES MUSEUM, KERMIT MUSEUM

Columbus•

Winterville Mounds State Historic Site
Leland•
Greenville•

Nanih Waiya Historic Site ▪

STATE CAPITOL, OLD CAPITOL MUSEUM OF MISSISSIPPI HISTORY

•Philadelphia

Alabama

Vicksburg National Military Park

Meridian•

Louisiana

Vicksburg• ⊗ Jackson

32°N

EMERALD MOUND, GRAND VILLAGE OF THE NATCHEZ INDIANS

Natchez

•Hattiesburg

N
W ⊕ E
S

0 20 40 miles
0 20 40 kilometers

STENNIS SPACE CENTER Gulfport•

OLD SPANISH FORT
Pascagoula
Biloxi•

Gulf Islands National Seashore

Gulf of Mexico

30°N

▲ **Places to visit in Mississippi**

mice scurry through the sands. Offshore, you might spot dolphins or whales. Hike along the winding nature trails. You'll discover alligators, opossums, and raccoons.

Natchez is the oldest permanent settlement on the Mississippi River. Dozens of plantation homes stand in the area. Visitors can tour many of the homes and gardens. Rosalie is the name of a mansion overlooking the river. It was the Union army's headquarters in Natchez during the Civil War.

▲ **The Auburn mansion in Natchez was built in 1812.**

Many ancient Native American mounds remain in Mississippi. Emerald Mound and Grand Village of the Natchez Indians are near Natchez. Emerald Mound is one of the United States' largest Native American mounds. Grand Village was a center for religious ceremonies. Winterville Mounds stands near Greenville.

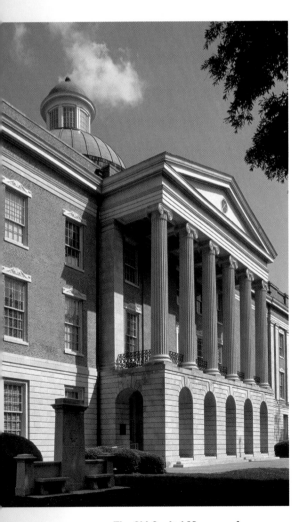

Its museum is full of fascinating objects found in the mounds. Nanih Waiya near Philadelphia is a holy mound for the Choctaw. According to legend, the tribe was born there.

The Old Capitol in Jackson was built in the 1830s. It now houses the Old Capitol Museum of Mississippi History. There, you'll explore Native American and pioneer life, the Civil War, and much more.

One of the Civil War's biggest battles took place at Vicksburg.

▲ **The Old Capitol Museum of Mississippi History in Jackson**

▲ **Graves at Vicksburg National Cemetery**

Today, you can see the battlefield's trenches and dozens of cannons. You'll also see the USS *Cairo,* a Civil War gunboat. Vicksburg National Cemetery contains thousands of soldiers' graves. Many other sites preserve Civil War battlefields. They include Tupelo, Brices Cross Roads, Corinth, and Champion Hill.

Highway 61 used to be called Blues Alley. Musicians who traveled this route created the famous Delta blues. You'll learn all about it at Clarksdale's Delta Blues Museum. The Highway 61 Blues Museum is in Leland, near Greenville.

Where was Kermit the Frog born? Kermit's creator, Jim Henson, said he was born in Leland on Deer Creek. Leland was Henson's hometown. Visit the exhibit in Leland dedicated

▲ Scenic Natchez Trace Parkway

to Kermit and his friends. You'll see a great collection of Muppet material.

Rock-and-roll king Elvis Presley came from Tupelo. Millions of visitors have toured the little house where he was born.

Tupelo is also the headquarters for the Natchez Trace Parkway. Take a drive along this winding, scenic highway. You'll see centuries of history pass before your eyes. This route began as a well-traveled Native American trail. Later, pioneers followed it through the wilderness. Bandits and robbers used the path, too!

Today, it passes Native American mounds, plantation sites, pioneer inns, and cemeteries. In some places, scientists are still digging up historic remains. They know what you've discovered yourself by now—Mississippi is an exciting place to explore!

Important Dates

1540–1541 Spanish explorer Hernando de Soto explores Mississippi and arrives at the Mississippi River.

1682 René-Robert Cavelier, Sieur de La Salle, claims all lands drained by the Mississippi River for France.

1699 Mississippi's first European settlement is established at Fort Maurepas (present-day Ocean Springs).

1716 Fort Rosalie (present-day Natchez) is founded.

1763 Mississippi comes under British rule.

1781 Spain gains control of southern Mississippi.

1783 Mississippi becomes U.S. territory, except for the Gulf Coast area.

1798 The Mississippi Territory is created.

1817 Mississippi becomes the twentieth U.S. state on December 10.

1861 Mississippi secedes from the Union and joins the Confederate States of America.

1862 Confederates lose the Battle of Corinth.

1863 Vicksburg surrenders to Union forces.

1864 Confederate general Nathan Bedford Forrest beats Union troops at Okolona and Brices Cross Roads.

1867 Reconstruction begins in Mississippi.

1907 Boll weevils destroy much of Mississippi's cotton crop.

1927 The Mississippi River floods, leaving thousands homeless.

1962 James Meredith is the first African-American to enter the University of Mississippi; federal troops subdue the resulting rioters.

1969 A federal court orders Mississippi schools to desegregate, or admit both blacks and whites.

1991 Kirk Fordice becomes Mississippi's first Republican governor since Reconstruction.

2000 Natchez celebrates the tricentennial, or 300th anniversary, of the French landing at Natchez.

Glossary

civil rights—the rights of each individual to freedom and equal treatment

Hispanic—people of Mexican, South American, and other Spanish-speaking cultures

indigo—a plant used to make a blue dye

industries—businesses or trades

integrated—accepting of all races

marshes—wetlands

mythical—imaginary or not real

plantations—large farms in the South, usually worked by slaves

Reconstruction—the period after the Civil War when the national government rebuilt the Union

virtual—providing an experience similar to real life

Did You Know?

★ The 1988 movie *Mississippi Burning* was based on the 1964 murders of three civil rights workers in Mississippi.

★ Walter Payton of Columbia was the first football player to appear on a box of Wheaties cereal.

★ Dr. James D. Hardy performed the first animal-to-human heart transplant at the University of Mississippi Medical Center in Jackson in 1964.

★ President Theodore Roosevelt was hunting bears in Mississippi in 1902. He refused to shoot at one bear that seemed tired and lame. News of this spread, and a toy maker began selling a stuffed bear called "Teddy's Bear." This is the origin of the teddy bear.

★ The world's oldest Holiday Inn is in Clarksdale.

State capital: Jackson

State motto: *Virtute et Armis* (Latin for "By Valor and Arms")

State nickname: Magnolia State

Statehood: December 10, 1817; twentieth state

Land area: 46,914 square miles (121,507 sq km); **rank:** thirty-first

Highest point: Woodall Mountain, 806 feet (246 m) above sea level

Lowest point: Sea level along the coast

Highest recorded temperature: 115°F (46°C) at Holly Springs on July 29, 1930

Lowest recorded temperature: −19°F (−28°C) at Corinth on January 30, 1966

Average January temperature: 46°F (8°C)

Average July temperature: 81°F (27°C)

Population in 2000: 2,844,658; **rank:** thirty-first

Largest cities in 2000: Jackson (184,256), Gulfport (71,127), Biloxi (50,644), Hattiesburg (44,779)

Factory products: Food products, transportation equipment, chemicals

Farm products: Chickens, cotton, soybeans

Mining products: Petroleum, natural gas

State flag: Mississippi's state flag has

three broad bars in the national colors —blue, white, and red. In the upper left-hand corner is a version of the flag of the Confederate States of America. It is a blue X against a field of red. Within the blue X are thirteen white stars. They stand for America's thirteen original colonies.

State seal: The state seal is a version of

the United States coat of arms. It shows an American eagle holding an olive branch and arrows in its claws. The olive branch is a symbol of peace. The arrows represent war. Together, they stand for the desire for peace along with the ability to go to war.

State abbreviations: Miss. (traditional); MS (postal)

State Symbols

State bird: Mockingbird

State flower: Magnolia blossom

State tree: Magnolia tree

State land mammal: White-tailed deer

State water mammal: Bottle-nosed dolphin

State waterfowl: Wood duck

State fish: Largemouth bass

State insect: Honeybee

State shell: Oyster shell

State stone: Petrified wood

State beverage: Milk

State fossil: Prehistoric whale

State commemorative quarter:
Released October 15, 2002

Making Mississippi Mud Pie

People say this pie looks like mud along the Mississippi riverbank!

Makes six to eight servings.

INGREDIENTS:

Filling:

1 cup powdered sugar

1 cup semisweet chocolate chips

¼ cup (½ stick) margarine

¼ cup whipping cream

2 tablespoons light corn syrup

1 teaspoon vanilla

2 pints coffee ice cream, divided

¾ cup chopped pecans, divided

Crust:

2 cups graham cracker crumbs

¼ cup sugar

½ cup (1 stick) margarine

DIRECTIONS:

Make sure an adult helps you with the hot stove. Blend the crust ingredients well and press into a 9-inch pie plate. For the filling, mix all the filling ingredients except the ice cream and nuts in a saucepan. Cook over low heat. Keep stirring until it's smooth. Pour one-third of this into the pie crust. Spread ¼ cup of the pecans on top. Spread 1 pint of ice cream on top of the pecans. Add another layer (same amounts) of chocolate mixture, nuts, and ice cream. Top with the rest of the chocolate, and sprinkle on the rest of the nuts. Put in the freezer for an hour before serving.

"Go, Mississippi"

Words and music by Houston Davis

States may sing their songs of praise
With waving flags and hip-hoo-rays,
Let cymbals crash and let bells ring
'Cause here's one song I'm proud to sing.

Choruses:
Go, Mississippi, keep rolling along,
Go, Mississippi, you cannot go wrong,
Go, Mississippi, we're singing your song,
M-I-S-S-I-S-S-I-P-P-I.

Go, Mississippi, you're on the right track,
Go, Mississippi, and this is a fact,
Go, Mississippi, you'll never look back,
M-I-S-S-I-S-S-I-P-P-I.

Go, Mississippi, straight down the line,
Go, Mississippi, ev'rything's fine,
Go, Mississippi, it's your state and mine,
M-I-S-S-I-S-S-I-P-P-I.

Go, Mississippi, continue to roll,
Go, Mississippi, the top is the goal,
Go, Mississippi, you'll have and you'll hold,
M-I-S-S-I-S-S-I-P-P-I.

Go, Mississippi, get up and go,
Go, Mississippi, let the world know,
That our Mississippi is leading the show,
M-I-S-S-I-S-S-I-P-P-I.

Famous Mississippians

Bo Diddley (1928–) is a blues and rock-and-roll guitarist. His real name is Elias McDaniel. He was born in McComb.

Charles Evers (1922–) is a civil rights leader. He was elected mayor of Fayette in 1969. He was Mississippi's first black elected official since Reconstruction. Medgar (below) was his brother. Evers was born in Decatur.

Medgar Evers (1925–1963) was a civil rights leader. He fought for voting rights and school integration. Evers was born in Decatur. He was shot and killed near his home in Jackson.

William Faulkner (1897–1962) wrote novels and short stories about life in the South. His books include *The Sound and the Fury* (1929) and *Go Down, Moses* (1942). Faulkner was born in New Albany.

Brett Favre (1969–) is a star quarterback with the Green Bay Packers football team. He was born in Gulfport.

Jim Henson (1936–1990) was a puppeteer. He invented Miss Piggy, Kermit the Frog, and the other Muppets. Henson was born in Greenville.

James Earl Jones (1931–) is an actor with a deep, resounding voice. He was born in Arkabutla.

B. B. King (1925–) is a blues guitarist and songwriter. He is often called the King of the Blues. "B. B." is short for "Blues Boy." His real first name is Riley. His guitar is named Lucille. King was born in Indianola.

Walter Payton (1954–1999) was a star football player for the Chicago Bears. He was nicknamed "Sweetness" for his smooth running style. Payton was born in Columbia.

Elvis Presley (1935–1977) was a wildly popular singer and actor. He is known as the King of Rock and Roll. Presley was born in Tupelo.

Leontyne Price (1927–) is a soprano singer and international opera star. She was born in Laurel.

William Grant Still (1895–1978) was a composer. His works include the *Afro-American Symphony* (1931). Still was born in Woodville.

Muddy Waters (1915–1983) was a blues singer and guitarist. He originated the Chicago blues style. His real name was McKinley Morganfield. He was born in Rolling Fork.

Eudora Welty (1909–2001) wrote novels and short stories. Her book *The Optimist's Daughter* (1972) won a Pulitzer Prize. Welty was born in Jackson.

Tennessee Williams (1911–1983) wrote plays. He won Pulitzer Prizes for *A Streetcar Named Desire* (1947) and *Cat on a Hot Tin Roof* (1955). Williams was born in Columbus.

Oprah Winfrey (1954–) is the host of the popular *Oprah Winfrey Show.* She received an Academy Award nomination for her role in the movie *The Color Purple* (1985). Winfrey (pictured above left) was born in Kosciusko.

At the Library

Elish, Dan. *James Meredith and School Desegregation.* Brookfield, Conn.: Millbrook, 1994.

Fireside, Harvey. *The "Mississippi Burning" Civil Rights Murder Conspiracy Trial.* Berkeley Heights, N.J.: Enslow, 2002.

Gilliland, Judith Heide, and Holly Meade (illustrator). *Steamboat: The Story of Captain Blanche Leathers.* New York: DK Publishing, 2000.

Joseph, Paul. *Mississippi.* Edina, Minn.: Abdo & Daughters, 1998.

Ready, Anna. *Mississippi.* Minneapolis: Lerner, 2002.

Thompson, Kathleen. *Mississippi.* Austin, Tex.: Raintree/Steck-Vaughn, 1996.

On the Web

Mississippi
http://www.mississippi.gov
To learn about Mississippi's government and economy

Mississippi Division of Tourism
http://www.visitmississippi.org
To find out about Mississippi's events, activities, and sights

Through the Mail

Mississippi Development Authority
Division of Tourism Development
P.O. Box 849
Jackson, MS 39205
For information on travel and interesting sights in Mississippi

Mississippi Department of Archives and History
P.O. Box 571
Jackson, MS 39205
For information on Mississippi's history

On the Road

Mississippi State Capitol
400 High Street
Jackson, MS 39201
601/359-3114
To visit Mississippi's state capitol

Index

About the Author

Ann Heinrichs grew up in Fort Smith, Arkansas, and lives in Chicago. She is the author of more than one hundred books for children and young adults on Asian, African, and U.S. history and culture. Ann has also written numerous newspaper, magazine, and encyclopedia articles. She is an award-winning martial artist, specializing in t'ai chi empty-hand and sword forms.

Ann has traveled widely throughout the United States, Africa, Asia, and the Middle East. In exploring each state for this series, she rediscovered the people, history, and resources that make this a great land, as well as the concerns we share with people around the world.